# THE
# HOPI
# INDIANS

THE JUNIOR LIBRARY OF
AMERICAN INDIANS

# THE
# HOPI
# INDIANS

*Bryan P. Sears*

CHELSEA JUNIORS

a division of CHELSEA HOUSE PUBLISHERS

FRONTISPIECE: A woman makes piki bread in the traditional fashion. Piki bread was served at both everyday meals and celebrations.

CHAPTER TITLE ORNAMENT: A kachina doll. Such dolls are given to Hopi children to represent the powerful spirits who play an important role in the Hopis' lives.

English-language words that are italicized in the text can be found in the glossary at the back of the book.

**Chelsea House Publishers**
EDITORIAL DIRECTOR  Richard Rennert
EXECUTIVE MANAGING EDITOR  Karyn Gullen Browne
COPY CHIEF  Robin James
PICTURE EDITOR  Adrian G. Allen
ART DIRECTOR  Robert Mitchell
MANUFACTURING DIRECTOR  Gerald Levine

**The Junior Library of American Indians**
SENIOR EDITOR  Ann-Jeanette Campbell

**Staff for THE HOPI INDIANS**
COPY EDITOR  Catherine Iannone
EDITORIAL ASSISTANT  Annie McDonnell
ASSISTANT DESIGNER  John Infantino
PICTURE RESEARCHER  Sandy Jones
COVER ILLUSTRATOR  Hal Just

First Printing

1  3  5  7  9  8  6  4  2

**Library of Congress Cataloging-in-Publication Data**

Sears, Bryan P.
The Hopi Indians / Bryan P. Sears.
  p.  cm. — (The Junior library of American Indians)
Includes index.
        0-7910-1662-5.
        0-7910-2487-3 (pbk.)
1. Hopi Indians—Juvenile literature. I. Title. II. Series.
E99.H7S33  1994                                          93-47541
973'.04974—dc20                                              CIP
                                                             AC

# CONTENTS

CHAPTER 1

# Dawn of the Hopis

Before there were people, animals, and land, there was nothing on earth except water. Two sister goddesses, each called Huruing Wuhti, lived in *kivas* (underground ceremonial rooms) in the oceans, one in the eastern ocean and one in the western. Huruing Wuhti means "Hard-Beings Woman." They were the goddesses of hard substances—such as rocks, clay, and minerals—beads, and precious objects—such as turquoise, seashells, and coral.

In each kiva, a ladder led to the opening in the roof. Two fox skins, one gray and one yellow, hung from the ladder in the eastern kiva. A turtle shell rattle hung from the ladder in the western kiva.

Each morning, in the eastern kiva, the sun put on the gray fox skin and climbed through the hole in the roof, causing the dawn of the Hopis. As he rose higher in the sky he put on the yellow skin, causing the day of the Hopis.

When the sun had completed his long journey across the sky, he announced his arrival to Huruing Wuhti of the West by shaking the turtle shell rattle tied to the ladder of her kiva. Then he continued his journey, underwater, back to the East.

Once, Huruing Wuhti of the West invited her sister to visit. At their meeting they pulled back the waters to leave a patch of dry land between their oceans. They then asked the sun to search this land for life as he traveled through the sky. The sun did as he was asked, but he could find nothing.

Perhaps the sun might have missed something to the north or south because he traveled only one path over the earth. Huruing Wuhti of the West again asked her sister to come to her kiva to talk. Huruing Wuhti of the East traveled over a rainbow to her sister's kiva in the West.

The goddess from the East made a small wren out of clay. She covered it with a piece of *mochapu,* or native cloth, and both goddesses sang over the clay figure, giving it life. The sisters sent the bird out into the world to search for life, but it also returned without finding any.

At this time another goddess, Kohkang Wuhti, which means "Spider Woman," lived in a kiva in the Southwest. The sun and the wren had not noticed her as they had searched for life.

Huruing Wuhti of the West created clay birds of many different types, and the goddesses sang them to life. They taught each bird the calls that it should make and sent them off in all different directions. The sisters made other animals in the same manner. Each was taught its own language before going out into the world.

The goddesses then decided to create human beings. Huruing Wuhti of the East first made a woman from clay and then a man and sang them both to life. She made two tablets, on which she drew characters with a wooden stick, and gave them to the man and woman. The humans could not read the writing on the tablets, so the goddess rubbed the palms of her hands against the palms of their hands. Then, they immediately understood. She taught them their language. The two humans then traveled across the rainbow to the kiva of

Huruing Wuhti of the East, where they stayed a short while before leaving with their children to live on the dry land.

When Spider Woman heard what the two sister goddesses were doing, she decided to create a man and a woman out of clay, too. She also sang them to life. But Spider Woman did not stop there. She created more and more men and women, and gave each pair a different language. She became tired, however, while making the humans and forgot to create a woman for one of the men. When she discovered her mistake, she made a woman and told her to go find the single man. If he did not accept her, she would have to live by herself. The woman found the man and he accepted her.

The man and the woman lived together peacefully for a time, but then they began to argue with each other. The woman decided that she wanted to live alone.

"I can cook for myself," she said.

"But who will get your wood and work the fields?" the man asked.

They decided to stay together, but they were constantly fighting with each other. If they had been able to get along, all Hopis would live in peace today.

Unfortunately, other couples learned from these two how to argue, and this is why there

*This two-year-old Hopi girl holds corn, crow mother, and sun kachina dolls, which represent important spirits of Hopi myths and history.*

are so many arguments, and not only between husbands and wives. Spider Woman's people were ill-mannered. When Huruing Wuhti of the West heard about them she summoned the goddess of the East for the third time.

"I do not want to live here alone. I want some good people around me," Huruing Wuhti of the West said.

She then created many pairs of peaceful people. These were the ancestors of the Hopis. They lived mostly by hunting rabbits, antelope, and deer for food and clothes. They followed as the animals moved in search of food, which is how they came to meet Spider Woman's people and learn how to argue.

As the years went by, the quarreling grew worse. Some of the people learned how to be mean and brutal. The good rain stopped. The land became *barren*.

The wisest chief held a council with the leaders of the good people. They decided that they must escape their world and find a better one. They prayed and smoked their pipes, but nothing came of it. They then asked Mockingbird and Yellow Bird for help. The birds took the shape of men, and they created an altar on which they put a ceremonial bowl of water ringed by four ears of

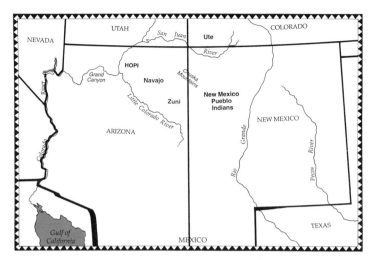

*In their creation story, the Hopi people emerged into the upper world in present-day Arizona and New Mexico; at least that is where evidence of their history begins.*

corn: yellow corn to the north, blue corn to the west, red corn to the south, and white corn to the east. They called upon Golden Eagle to fly high to find a way out of the earth. But he did not find one.

The wise councillors called bird after bird, but none was successful until they called the songbird Shrike. While Shrike searched the sky, the councillors prayed and smoked their pipes. Shrike returned with news of a small hole far, far up in the sky.

Shrike suggested calling upon Chipmunk to plant a tree that would grow quickly and take the people up to the hole. First Chipmunk planted a spruce tree, but it did not grow tall enough. Tree after tree he planted, but not one was tall enough. Then, Chipmunk brought to the altar a cutting of a hollow reed and the tiny shell of a piñon nut filled with water. After he prayed and sang and smoked his pipe, he planted the cutting. From it sprang a reed that grew quickly. Chipmunk ran up it and pulled on the reed's top to encourage it to grow further.

Grow it did. It grew until it reached right through the hole in the sky, at the place now called *shipapu*. The chief and his councillors brought their families to the reed, and one by one they climbed up its hollow inside until they got to the upper world. There they settled.

This myth about the creation of the under-world and the journey of the Hopis to the upper world is one of many stories meant to teach about the Hopi way of life. For instance, because it tells how the world came to be so quarrelsome, it suggests how highly the Hopis value harmony.

The animals, spirits, and wonderful details that fill the Hopi creation story make it not only educational but entertaining. The story brings to life the ancient mythological world of the Hopis. ▲

*Second Mesa—one of three mesas where there are modern-day Hopi towns—displays the formidable landscape where descendants of the Anasazi Tradition made their homes.*

CHAPTER 2

# The Prehistoric
# Traditions

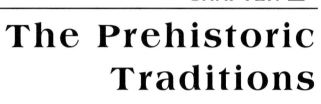

The history of the Hopis extends back at least 10,000 years, long before the first Europeans set foot on the North American continent. The Hopis' ancestors lived in what is now the southwestern United States, a harsh but beautiful place.

The land is made up of deserts, *mesas,* deep canyons, and towering *plateaus.* The lack of rain and flowing water makes survival very difficult, but the region is capable of sustaining plant and animal life. Juniper and piñon trees dot the landscape, growing there along with many types of grasses, roots, and cacti. Rabbits, small desert rodents, and

*Prehistoric corn is one of the puzzle pieces studied today to get a clearer understanding of life during the Desert, Mogollon, and Anasazi traditions.*

reptiles are also native to the Southwest. Larger creatures, such as deer, antelope, and bear, roam the mountains there.

Experts divide the prehistory of the native people of this region into three separate periods, called traditions: the Desert Tradition, the Mogollon Tradition, and the Anasazi Tradition.

Campsites belonging to the people of the Desert Tradition have been found at Concho in eastern Arizona and at Bat Cave and Tularosa Cave in New Mexico. These people lived about 10,000 years ago. They were nomadic, on the move gathering plants and hunting wild animals for their food instead of settling permanently, growing crops and raising herds of animals. When they had used up the food supply in one area, they would move to another. Their camps were small, consisting of only a few families which would move from area to area together.

Desert people hunted not only smaller animals but great bison and ancestors of the modern-day elephant, once abundant in North America. These animals provided materials for clothing, utensils, and shelter as well as food.

For thousands of years, Desert people *foraged* in order to survive. Then they learned to grow corn, which became a sacred symbol as well as a practical crop. Corncobs dating back about 5,000 years have been found at some of their prehistoric campsites. The Desert people invented grinding stones called *metates* for grinding corn, seeds, and nuts.

At first, and for almost 2,000 years, corn was the only crop grown by Desert people.

Through a process called cultural diffusion, in which one culture passes on its knowledge to a neighboring culture, the Hopis' ancestors learned additional farming methods from people living in central Mexico. This added squash and beans to their crops and their diet. Corn, squash, and beans have been the basis of native southwestern cooking ever since. Despite their increased knowledge of farming, Desert people continued to live as nomads.

The Mogollon Tradition began approximately 2,000 years ago and marked a radical change from the Desert Tradition. Mogollon people settled in permanent villages with houses built out of clay and stone instead of moving around in search of food. The population in each of the settlements numbered about 100 people.

The Mogollon people made earthen pottery of many sizes and shapes for cooking and storing food and supplies. They invented the bow and arrow for hunting and the *mortar and pestle* for grinding plant foods by hand.

With the start of the Anasazi Tradition, around A.D. 1100, larger settlements began to spring up in the region of the Southwest now called the Four Corners, where Arizona, New Mexico, Utah, and Colorado meet. Anasazi people built rectangular houses up to three stories high along their towns' streets, plazas, and courtyards. Today, ruins of the impressive Anasazi settlements can be seen in Canyon de Chelly and Kayenta in Arizona, Mesa Verde in Colorado, and Chaco Canyon in New Mexico.

The Anasazi people developed two ways of securing the much-needed, but scarce, water for their farms. They planted crops near streams that overflowed after heavy rains and they redirected streams to *irrigate* their fields.

Then, sometime in the 14th century the Anasazi people suddenly abandoned their larger towns, probably because of a drastic change in the climate. The region became even more *arid* than before, and water became harder to find. People began to form smaller communities, which developed into individual tribes, including the Hopis.

While many of these new tribes moved to other parts of the Southwest, particularly to the Rio Grande valley, the Hopis remained in the desert lands of present-day Arizona. Most Hopis lived in villages near Kayenta and Black Mesa. Severe droughts between 1350 and 1450 caused the Hopis at the Kayenta site to relocate to the Hopi villages of Black Mesa. This brought the village populations to between 500 and 1,000 people.

Farming became the major occupation of the Hopis, and the village sites were conducive to the work. The strong winds blew sand from the mesas onto Hopi lands, forming *dunes,* and crops benefited because dunes retain water. The Hopis also built wind breaks out of brush and stone to protect the plants from being damaged by the winds.

The Hopis had already developed new kinds of corn and beans, specifically adapted to the arid climate. These plants had roots that could reach down 15 to 20 feet into the soil. This protected them from being pulled up by the winds and allowed them to absorb more of the moisture in the ground.

Not only agricultural advances marked this period. While all people living in the area made pottery, the Hopis' designs began to change dramatically. Previously their pottery had white backgrounds painted with black geometric shapes. Sometime in the 14th century, Hopi women started using a variety of color combinations, such as black on orange or black on yellow, and multicolored decorations. This burst of artistry also added sweeping curved lines and naturalistic images of people and animals to the more traditional geometric shapes.

In preparation for religious ceremonies, Hopi artists painted the walls of the kivas with

*When the Anasazi suddenly left their cliff dwellings in the 14th century, they moved to smaller towns similar to Mishongnovi, shown here in 1901.*

colorful pictures of people and events in Hopi myths. When the ceremony was over, the painting was covered with a fresh coat of plain plaster. This clean surface would be painted for the next ceremony. At a Hopi settlement called Awatovi, the walls of a kiva have been discovered to have 100 layers of plaster—30 of them with paintings.

Coal mining was another important development of 14th-century Hopi culture. Coal

*This kiva painting was found in Awatovi, where the walls of one kiva had 100 layers of plaster, 30 of them with paintings.*

was used by the Hopis for heating, firing pottery, and cooking (to get rid of the *noxious* fumes given off by burning coal, they developed chimneys to channel the fumes outdoors). They also used coal for coloring ceramics and paintings. In building, to lay a stone floor, coal ash was put down and the flagstones were set on top of it.

The Hopis acquired their coal mostly by strip-mining, now a controversial method because it destroys soil for agriculture. In strip-mining, surface soil and rock is removed and the coal underneath is dug out. The Hopis also developed underground mines to get at coal deep beneath the earth's surface. It is believed that at Awatovi, the Hopis removed about 450 pounds of coal a day, almost 30,000 tons over a period of 300 years.

By the start of the 16th century, when Spanish invaders arrived, the Southwest was dotted with the villages of the many different peoples descended from the Anasazi. These tribes had distinct cultures and separate languages, but the Spanish did not distinguish between them. They called all the tribes Pueblos—"villages" in Spanish—including the Hopis.

There were also tribes in the region that were not Pueblos. The Pimas, Papagos, and Havasupais were farming tribes friendly with the Hopis. Other tribes—especially the Utes and the Navajos—occasionally raided the Hopi villages, taking crops, domestically raised turkeys, and other goods. In spite of these raids, the Hopis traded with them when necessary.

Having lived for centuries in their communities, rich with history and culture, the Hopis considered themselves safe and secure in their ancient homeland. ▲

Corn is a sacred symbol
in Hopi culture. Women
have the responsibility
of grinding it on metates,
or grinding stones; each
house has a different
metate for coarse,
medium, and fine grinds.

# CHAPTER 3

# The Peaceful People

The word *Hopi* is an abbreviation of the phrase *Hopituh Shi-nu-mu,* which means "the peaceful people." The Hopis have traditionally based their lives on harmony and balance, believing that everyone should be kind and generous to others.

Before the Spanish arrived in the 16th century, there were six main towns, including Awatovi, and a few smaller villages. The population of the towns was small because the farmland could support only limited numbers of people. The Hopis depended primarily on rainfall to water their crops. Because the dry, desert climate did not always provide enough rain, there were years of drought.

None of the Hopi towns had a formal system of political government or written laws. Instead, every Hopi belonged to both a family and a clan, which protected their own members and made sure they acted responsibly in the community. Families were matrilineal, tracing their ancestry through the mother, and Hopis automatically belonged to the same clan as their mother.

The family included many relatives: an elder woman, her husband, her unmarried children, and her married daughters with their husbands and children. A married daughter remained with her own family. A married son went to live with his wife's family but kept close ties to his own sisters and mother. It was his job, for instance, to discipline his sister's children.

Everyone was expected to help with family tasks and to look after one another's children. The large number of relatives might live together in one house or build houses near the eldest woman's house.

The eldest woman in the family was always the head of the household. She advised family members and planned family events. Her eldest daughter also carried great influence within the family, and upon her

*Every Hopi belongs to a clan, and each clan has its own symbol. Shown here are the symbols of the major clans of Shongopovi including the eagle, snow, spider, antelope, and corn clans.*

mother's death, she would become the head of the household.

One of the eldest woman's responsibilities was to take care of ceremonial objects belonging to the family. The most important of these was a sacred piece of corn, which represented the family. Wrapped in feathers and cloth, it was usually placed on a special altar made just for it.

Even now, a Hopi child automatically belongs to his or her mother's clan. Clans are large groups of people—numbering into the hundreds—who consider themselves related, although no trace of blood kinship may be found. The Hopi clans took their names from nature: birds, such as sparrow and hawk; mammals, reptiles, and insects, such as bear, lizard, and butterfly; food, such

*The chiefs of the Walpi, Hano, and Sichomovi pueblos gathered for this photograph sometime between 1880 and 1882.*

as corn and squash; and plants and substances, such as cactus and sand.

The Hopis' philosophy of kindness and generosity to others applied especially among clan members. Clan members lent economic and emotional assistance to one another and helped one another in times of emergency.

The eldest woman in the clan was the clan mother. She advised on clan matters and settled any disputes that arose. When the clan mother died, the next oldest woman succeeded her. The brother of the clan mother was also a member of importance. His opinion carried a great deal of weight and it was his responsibility to organize clan ceremonies.

Individual Hopis did not own land, but instead, the clan mother gave the head of each household a portion of land for farming. Because the climate made farming so difficult in the Southwest, a household's land was not all in one place. Pockets of land in different areas were given out so that at least some of the crops would have a chance to succeed. The plots were marked in the corners with stones painted to represent the clan that farmed the land.

In addition to family and clan leaders, each village had its own town chief, called a *kikmongwi,* or "leader of the house." The kikmongwi's most important responsibilities were the ceremonies and rituals involving the whole village.

Elected by the village clan leaders, the kikmongwi held his position for life. He had to be an even-tempered man belonging to the bear clan, a good farmer, and a respected member of his family and community. The kikmongwi was expected to keep himself removed from the day-to-day squabbles of life and to concentrate instead on spiritual matters. If he became arrogant, abusive, or incompetent, he could be removed by the clan leaders.

The town crier was a special assistant to the kikmongwi. At the kikmongwi's request, he would climb to the top of one of the houses in the center of town to make announcements regarding such subjects as important *ritual* events or a planting season.

Hopi men and women were taught different tasks and responsibilities. The division of labor was based on sex, but each person's work was considered equally valuable. Traditionally, relationships between men and women were based on the Hopi philosophy of balance and give-and-take.

In general, men had responsibility for work performed outside of the home. As the farmers of the family, they first worked with their male relatives on the land given to their mothers. After they married they worked on the land given to their wives.

The Hopis grew several kinds of corn, including blue, white, and sweet corn. The first corn was planted in April and harvested in mid-July for the *Kachina Niman* ceremony. (This ceremony marks when the kachinas, or "spirit beings," return to their mountain homes after their annual six-month visit with the Hopis.) In May, more corn was planted along with beans and squash. These crops were harvested in the late summer and early autumn. The Hopis planted tobacco as well, and cotton which was woven to make clothing and blankets.

*This Hopi woman in her bridal garments holds a reed case made to store them. Traditionally, her intended husband would weave the cloth for her wedding outfit.*

Men hunted for food too, using wooden bows and arrows tipped with stone arrowheads. Close to home they hunted small animals, but sometimes they traveled into the mountains to hunt larger game, such as antelope and deer.

Farming and hunting tools were made by the men, as were shields and weapons for battle and woven baskets for storing food. Men cut firewood for heating and cooking and made beautiful jewelry out of turquoise, shells, and coral.

Hopi women's tasks revolved around the home: cleaning, making pottery, preparing food, and plastering the cracks in the walls.

Grinding corn—the main ingredient of the Hopis' diet—was one of the most important jobs of Hopi women. Every home had three metates, or grinding stones. The difference between the three was how finely each ground the corn.

The women used a piki stone to cook one of the most prized Hopi foods: piki bread. Piki bread was made by pouring a thin batter of blue cornmeal onto the stone after it had been oiled and heated. When cooked, the piki bread was folded or rolled before it cooled. It was served at daily meals as well as at ceremonies.

When a Hopi man and woman married, one of the ceremonial traditions had the bride go to her mother-in-law's home for four days before the marriage. While there, she would grind corn and make piki bread to be served at the wedding meal. At the same time, the groom went to a kiva with his male relatives and spun cotton into cloth to be used for wedding clothes.

Traditionally, for everyday clothes, men wore cotton shirts and aprons over deerskin leggings, and women wore blouses and skirts. Sometimes the clothing was brightly embroidered and decorated with sashes, tassels, and jewelry made from turquoise and shells. Hopis protected their feet with moccasins and boots made from antelope or deer hide.

Children learned the values that guided the Hopis at an early age. Until they were two years old, they would be showered with attention, affection, and indulgence. After that, the child became accountable for his or her own actions. The traditions of harmony, kindness, generosity, respect, and helpfulness were joined by the goals of an even temper, restraint from anger or argument, and acceptance of discomfort and displeasure without complaint.

The family and community both played important roles in disciplining children. Several times a year two men wearing masks would go through the village in search of children who had misbehaved. Parents watched for these men and, when they were spotted, told their children to run and hide. If their children had been very bad, the parents told the men where to find them. Once found, they were given lectures or whippings.

The Hopis believed a wrongful act or thought could make a person ill. Disease resulted when a person's internal peace and harmony were disturbed. To stay well, one had to have a "good heart," as reflected in one's thoughts and actions. When the inner balance was out of kilter, a Hopi would seek the help of a man or a woman known to be a healer. A healer might use plants and roots that have natural medicines within them or might treat the problem by performing a ritual, calling on spirits and praying for the return of the person's "good heart."

Despite the harsh climate and occasional raids by other tribes, until the 16th century the Hopis led secure lives, enriched by their own traditional values. With the arrival of the Spanish *conquistadores,* however, the values and security of "the peaceful people" became threatened with extinction. ◣

El Señor D. Diego de
Brazos Zapata Lujan, Pon
ze de Leon, Marques de la Na
ba de Barcinas, del Orden de
S. tiago, Governador, Conquis
tador, Pacificador, y Capitan
General del Nueko Mejico, ex
pendio la Vida en Campaña
Rasa por libertar la Patria
en 16 de madzo en el Sitio
de Bernalillo año
de MDCCIV

Este cuadro, que el Instituto de Cultura Hispanica ofrece al Museo de Nuebo Mejico, es co-
pia del verdadero retrato de D. Diego Brazos Zapata, de la Casa de los Vargas, cuyo original se
conserva en la capilla de San Isidro sita en el Pueblo de Zantistaban del Madrid.

*In 1692, Don Diego de Vargas led Spanish forces against the Hopis to recapture towns and territory they had lost to the Indians 12 years earlier.*

CHAPTER 4

# The Spanish Expeditions

In 1539, a Spanish priest named Marcos de Niza returned to Mexico from a trip north—into what is now New Mexico and Arizona—telling tales of golden treasure and wealthy cities to be found there. The Spanish had recently conquered the powerful Aztecs in Mexico and wanted to expand their empire further. On his trip, Niza, in fact, had not set foot in any Pueblo village, but his fabulous tales sent the Spanish northward, hungry for more conquests.

The first Spanish expedition of soldiers and priests, led by Francisco Vásquez de Coronado, arrived on foot and horseback in

what is now New Mexico in 1540. Coronado quickly set up headquarters in the village of Tiguex. From there, he sent out expeditions to settlements along the Rio Grande and in Arizona. Pedro de Tovar was sent with 20 soldiers and one priest to the Hopi village of Awatovi.

When the Spanish came to the Southwest, they identified all the native peoples as Pueblos, from the Spanish word *pueblo*, which means village. (Pueblos, when capitalized, refers to the people and, when lowercase, refers to their villages.)

*Seeking towns rumored to have great wealth, Francisco Vásquez de Coronado led the first Spanish expedition into Pueblo and Hopi territory.*

The Spanish did not distinguish between the Tewas, the Lagunas, the Hopis, or the many other peoples living in separate villages. While these native Indian groups shared qualities in general, they differed sharply in such important ways as language and cultural identity. The peoples lived close to each other, but they thought of themselves as separate nations—especially the Hopi who lived on the outskirts of Pueblo territory in what is now Arizona. The Spanish, however, lumped all the Indians together under the name *Pueblos.*

At first, the Pueblos welcomed the Spaniards to their villages. They traded freely with them, obtaining metal tools in exchange for food and clothing. Soon, however, the Spanish visitors began to demand more.

In Tiguex, Coronado's base, the relationship between the residents and the foreigners grew increasingly worse, to the point where the Indians tried, unsuccessfully, to expel the Spanish from the village. Pueblo bows and arrows were no match for Spanish guns. When Coronado ordered the execution of several hundred natives in response to the uprising, word of the brutality spread quickly among the Pueblos. From that time on, the Spanish were viewed as dangerous enemies.

Hopi villages were not *exempt* from suffering. Along with other Pueblos, when they learned of the cruelties in Tiguex, they refused to cooperate with the Spanish. In return, the Spanish ordered beatings, torture, and executions.

A Spanish witness in one pueblo described the brutality of his countrymen:

> the corners of the pueblo were taken by four men and four others began to seize the natives who showed themselves. As the pueblo was large and the majority hid themselves, we set fire to the big pueblo, where we thought some were burned to death because of the cries that they uttered. We at once took out prisoners, two at a time, and lined them up, where they were shot many times until they were dead. Sixteen were executed not counting those who were burned to death.

By the late 1500s the Spanish government began setting up permanent colonies in the Pueblos' territory. In 1598 the first governor, Juan de Oñate, made his headquarters in a pueblo in New Mexico. He soon began to make heavy demands of the village inhabitants, and he responded to any resistance with the same cruel methods as Coronado.

Every month, soldiers rode into the various pueblos to take the people's corn and blankets. The Pueblos wept and cried as if they were being slaughtered, for in this land of hardship, the theft of such essentials had severe repercussions.

*Spanish priests forced the Hopis not only to accept Christianity but to build churches. If the Hopis refused, the priests could have them whipped, tortured, or even killed.*

Even the Spanish authorities in Mexico considered Oñate's actions outrageous. In 1607 he was replaced by Pedro de Peralta, who moved the capital of his administration to the pueblo of Santa Fe. Peralta was no better than Oñate. He forced the people of Santa Fe to build a palace and other buildings for his government and to surrender food and blankets as *tribute.* Some Indians were enslaved in Spanish mines or forced to work as servants.

Throughout Pueblo territory, Spanish priests forced villagers to build churches and to abandon their native religious practices and beliefs in favor of Christianity. In the process, the priests destroyed many ritual objects and works of art.

The priests also confiscated land and used Pueblo labor to grow crops. They then sold the surplus crops to government officials, soldiers, and settlers for enormous profits. Resistance to the priests resulted in more brutality and death.

Among the Hopis, the first *mission* was established in the town of Awatovi, in 1609. Led by Francisco Porras, the priests tried to convert the Hopis to Christianity, with little success.

Porras, however, was not as cruel as the other priests. He even tried to learn the Hopi language so that he could speak directly to the Hopis. Most priests used bilingual native interpreters because church authorities in Mexico believed that if a priest learned to speak the native tongue, he might sympathize with the natives' complaints.

The Spanish continued to force the natives to convert, to provide labor, and to give up their food and supplies. But they also introduced many new tools, crops, and jobs to the Hopis: metal axes and shovels; peaches, melons, and tomatoes; and raising

*continued on page 49*

# SPIRITS AND GODS

The Hopis understand that to be truly well, they must have "good hearts." This means being kind, generous, good-natured, and respectful of the natural world. For the Hopis, everything—plants, animals, humans, even clouds—has a spirit, and honoring these spirits creates balance and harmony in the individual, in society, and in the world. Kachinas represent these spirits in the form of costumed characters at rituals, paintings on kiva walls, and the special kachina dolls given to children.

The Hopi year is divided into the months when the kachinas visit the villages at major religious ceremonies and the months when they have returned to their homes. Hopis give thanks and praise to the kachinas, and, in turn, the kachinas carry their messages and prayers to the spirits. Sometimes the kachinas leave gifts of kachina dolls for children, but these are not toys. Instead they are given a special place in the home and are treasured as small parts of the spirits themselves.

Kachinas may appear to be frightening, beautiful, or clownish, but they are all powerful spirits who give support to the Hopis in return for the Hopis' loyalty. In this way, balance and harmony in the world is maintained.

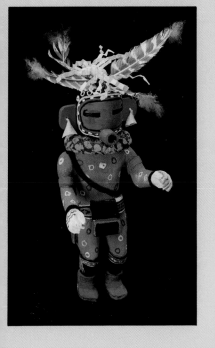

*This Hopi kachina doll represents Avatshoya.*
*A kachina might be named after the animal or spirit it represents, the kind of noise it makes, the way it moves, or some other aspect of its character.*

*Kuwan Powamu Koyemsi is a* Kooyemsi, *or mudhead kachina. No one knows exactly how many different kachinas there are in Hopi religious belief, particularly because certain kachinas appear only in certain villages.*

Mastopkatsina would visit Oraibi during
Soyalangw, the ceremony that marked
the winter solstice, or as the Hopi said,
the return of the sun to its winter house.
Many of the rituals performed during
Soyalangw are concerned with fertility
and preparations for the upcoming
planting season.

Pawiki is a duck kachina.

43

*Tsorporyaqahontaqa (with the blue face) and Eewero are* kipokkatsinam, *or raider kachinas. At the end of Hopi dances, the* kipokkatsinam *punish the* tsuskut, *or Hopi clowns, for their un-Hopi-like behavior.*

*Kisa is a prairie falcon kachina.*

*Hilili is a kachina doll carved in a simple, traditional style. Traditional kachinas were carved from the root of a cottonwood tree. The Hopi call kachinas carved in this style* ponotutuyqa, *or one with a stomachache, referring to the arms clasped over the belly.*

*Kweo, the wolf kachina.*

*Nata'aska is a black ogre kachina. During the Powamuy, or Bean Dance, ceremony, such ogres go from house to house reciting the misdeeds of the children who live within and threatening to kidnap or eat them.*

*continued from page 40*

sheep and cattle. Unfortunately, the priests and the soldiers also brought with them new diseases, against which the Hopis had no *antibodies.*

The middle of the 17th century brought hardships to the Hopi villages. All of the Pueblos suffered not only the Spanish tyranny but also droughts, raids, and epidemics. Enormous numbers of people died from smallpox and measles carried by the Spanish. Whole households were wiped out and few, if any, families were left untouched.

The Hopis believed that the balance of their universe had been disturbed with the arrival of the Europeans. And the foreigners' attempt to root out Hopi native beliefs had violated the sacred relationships between the Hopis and their spiritual protectors. Although the Hopis feared massive retaliation if they resisted the Spanish demands, they grew more and more unwilling to bear the disruption of their harmonious life.

In the summer of 1680, Pueblo leaders from many towns met in secret and decided to rid themselves of their Spanish overlords. The most prominent of the leaders was a Tewa chief named Popé. The Spanish had once accused him of witchcraft and had punished him with a public whipping.

Popé and the other delegates planned to blockade Santa Fe, the Spanish headquarters, in order to stop supplies from going in. They knew when the Spanish would be low on food and other necessary goods and expecting a new shipment. The plan was to cut off the supplies, forcing the Spanish to leave. Additionally, the leaders coordinated attacks on the Spanish soldiers and priests in their various villages.

The siege was to begin August 11, 1680. On August 9, the two messengers chosen to carry final plans to the pueblos were arrested. It seemed that the Spanish governor, Antonio de Otermin, had heard about the revolt in advance. Popé decided to attack immediately.

The Pueblos succeeded in cutting off supplies and water to Santa Fe and in killing the soldiers and priests in the villages. The Hopis killed the priests in their villages and destroyed the churches they had been forced to build. Otermin realized he was beaten. The Spanish started to leave Pueblo territory and, at that point, the Pueblos allowed them to leave in peace. By August 21, the Spanish were gone.

Peace lasted for a short 12 years before Spanish commander Diego de Vargas

*When the Spanish returned in 1692, only the Hopis of Awatovi let them build a mission—similar to this one in Acoma Pueblo, New Mexico—on their land again.*

marched into Pueblo territory and began to reimpose control over the villages. Vargas headed toward Hopi land, but when he got there he found that the Hopis had moved to the tops of three mesas.

Vargas tried to attack but failed to enter any of the settlements. The tops of the mesas were reachable by only one path, which protected the villages. In addition to this natural defense, the Hopis received help from Ute and Navajo Indians, who raided the Spanish soldiers before they reached the mesas.

The Spanish continued to send military expeditions to force the Hopis to submit, but these attacks always failed. The village of Awatovi, however, allowed Spanish priests to build another church on Hopi land.

Understandably, most Hopis were outraged. They believed that the priests' return would bring back the former Spanish terrors. Hopi leaders outside of Awatovi tried unsuccessfully to convince the leaders there to throw the priests out. In 1701 a clan chief named Espeleta led a Hopi attack against Awatovi. All of the men in the town were killed and the women and children were forced to leave. From then on, the Hopis kept the conquistadores out of Hopi towns.

The Spanish were not the only problem that beset the Hopis in the 18th century. In 1777 severe drought hit the region, bringing with it crop failure and famine. Increased Navajo raids made the Hopis' struggle for survival even more difficult.

The end of the century, however, brought a period of rebuilding to the Hopis. Hopi villages were far from the center of the Spanish government, which meant that military campaigns against the natives would be costly and dangerous. In 1821, Mexico won independence from Spain, and the Hopis—along with the rest of the Pueblos—were given full Mexican citizenship. It didn't matter much to them, however. They were too far away from the seat of the Mexican government to be troubled by it.

They were finally left alone. This isolation allowed the Hopis to restore themselves; to concentrate on their families, communities, and crops; and to work toward peace, harmony, and balance in the universe. ⊼

*In 1894–95, these Hostiles, who actively fought against the U.S. government's policies, were arrested and sent to prison on Alcatraz for seven months.*

# CHAPTER 5

# The Americans

The early 1800s marked the appearance of the first Americans in what would become the American Southwest. Trappers and traders came in search of beavers, whose pelts were in great demand both in the United States and in Europe. Once the Santa Fe Trail was opened—connecting the Southwest with eastern cities—the town of Santa Fe bustled with trading activity.

While the Hopis continued to isolate themselves from newcomers and outsiders, contact did occur, and sometimes it was *tainted* with violence. One such case, in 1840, involved a group of trappers employed by the Rocky Mountain Fur Company. The trappers

looted a number of Hopi farms and then attacked a group of Hopis who tried to approach them, killing between 15 and 20 people.

The Southwest, including the ancestral home of the Hopis, became part of the United States at the end of the Mexican-American War (1846–48). Under the 1848 Treaty of Guadalupe Hidalgo, Mexico gave up this territory to the U.S. government in return for its promise to treat all former Mexican citizens with respect. Unfortunately, the U.S. government did not consider any of the Pueblos to be citizens. They were defined as *wards* of the government and lost their equal status with Hispanic and Anglo residents. They had

*Fort Defiance, Arizona, was built to protect newly arrived American citizens as much as to fulfill the U.S. government's promise to help defend the Hopis against Navajo raids.*

to trust the U.S. government for protection, which proved unreliable.

The U.S. Bureau of Indian Affairs (BIA) appointed John Calhoun as the agent who would oversee the southwest territory. When he set up regional headquarters for the BIA in Santa Fe in 1850, Hopi leaders went to meet with him, seeking good relations with the new government. They asked Calhoun for help to stop the increasing number of Navajo raids on their villages.

Calhoun gave the leaders presents and a promise to help stop the raids. The government kept this promise, building Fort Defiance in Arizona and sending troops to fight the raiders. Perhaps the U.S. government was ready to act on behalf of the Hopis' welfare after all. Calhoun's action, however, benefited the new American settlers as much as the Hopis, and it is possible that concern for the settlers' safety motivated the government's prompt response.

Further droughts and epidemics—which reduced the Hopi population by as much as 75 percent—and increased Navajo raids caused the Hopi leaders to look again to the U.S. government for help. But the government was too busy fighting the Civil War to offer any assistance. By the time troops returned to the southwest territory in 1864, the entire Hopi tribe numbered no more than 3,000 people.

When they had returned, U.S. forces once again responded to the Hopis' need for help against the Navajos, but they acted in the best interests of the United States, not the Native Americans. The U.S. government not only wanted to control the native population, it wanted the freedom to mine Indian territory. Coming to the aid of the Hopis gave the U.S. government an excuse to force the Navajos off their native land, land which it believed was rich in gold and precious minerals.

Fighting the Navajos, U.S. soldiers killed hundreds, and maybe thousands, of men, women, and children. In addition to the massive death count, 8,000 Navajos were brutally marched 250 miles from their homeland and imprisoned at Bosque Redondo, New Mexico. This torturous journey is still remembered as the Long Walk. The Hopis once again felt safe, but this safety came at the expense of Navajo lives and land.

In 1870 the BIA opened the Hopi Indian Agency in the Hopi town of Oraibi and four years later established a second agency in Keams Canyon. (Keams Canyon was a town that had been founded by a family of Anglo traders.) Railroads began to bring more and more Anglos into the southwest territory. Workers and settlers came, followed by missionaries: Baptists, Moravians, Mennonites, and Mormons. More towns of non-Indians sprang up, and the Mormons and Moravians built missions and settlements near Hopi villages. Soon these settlers began *encroaching* on Hopi lands.

In 1882, President Chester Arthur responded to Hopi appeals for help by signing an executive order. Instead of moving the Hopis onto a reservation, which is what happened to many other tribes, the U.S. government turned 2.5 million acres of Hopi land into a reservation. The order specified that the land was to be inhabited only by "Hopis and other Indians." This wording would become vitally important in the next century.

Hopi contact with the newcomers was neither all bad nor all good. Between the departure of the Spanish from Hopi territory and the arrival of the Americans, the Hopis had lived by themselves, their way of life essentially unchanged. From the settlers, the Hopis now adopted new farming technology, such as the use of plows and iron hoes. They also added wooden doors and glass windows to their houses. But U.S. government policies soon threatened the balance which was a goal of traditional Hopi society.

The U.S. government ordered schools to be opened for Hopi children. In 1874 a school was started at Keams Canyon (not until later were schools opened in Hopi villages). Some Hopis wanted their children to learn the English language and American ways, but others strongly opposed enforced schooling. They were sure that the children would forget the traditional ways and that, as a result, the balance and harmony so important to the Hopi people would be disturbed.

The government tried to persuade the reluctant parents to send their children to school by giving them gifts of shovels, axes, and rakes. When this bribery did not work, troops were sent to round up the children and take them to school by force. Fathers who kept their children at home were sentenced to 30 days of hard labor. (In her autobiography, Helen Sekaquaptewa remembers when she was a young Hopi student seeing her father and other prisoners walk by the schoolyard on their way to the labor camp. The prisoners were connected two by two with a ball and chain.) In 1890 troops entered a kiva during an initiation rite for boys. They interrupted the ceremony and simply took all the boys away.

*In 1874, this school at Keams Canyon was opened, and Hopi children were forced to attend. At that time, the school's goal seemed to be to strip the students of their tribal identity.*

These actions helped to inflame an already angry Hopi population. The Anglos did not stop there. Teachers and missionaries persuaded the government to ban Hopi religious ceremonies. The U.S. government ruled that constitutional freedom of religion did not apply to Native Americans. The ruling only caused the Hopis to hold their ceremonies in secret.

American interference in Hopi society split the tribe into two factions. The two opposing groups were known as the Friendlies and the Hostiles. Friendlies wanted to cooperate with the U.S. government. Most of them

were bilingual and already had daily contact with Anglos. The Hostiles viewed the Anglo newcomers as a threat to their existence. Among other concerns, they resented the enforcement of government policies—such as the education of Hopi children—without their being consulted first.

Conflict erupted between the Friendlies and the Hostiles in the Hopi village of Shongopovi. There, Hostiles refused to allow American health workers to give smallpox vaccinations. Friendlies in Shongopovi then forced the Hostiles to leave the village, but that did not stop the feuding. In fact, it only became worse.

*Yokeoma, a Hostile leader from Hotevilla, was arrested in 1906 because he opposed enforced school attendance and other U.S. governmental policies. Here he is taken away after being arrested.*

The Hostiles from Shongopovi moved to Oraibi, which already had its own fighting factions. The arguments became so severe that the Friendlies and Hostiles could no longer interact with each other. They even began holding rituals in separate kivas.

The two sides found it impossible to agree with each other, with one exception: they agreed that one group had to leave. On September 8, 1906, a tug-of-war was held to determine who would stay and who would leave. A rope was laid on the ground. The Friendlies gathered on one side of a line drawn in the dirt, and the Hostiles gathered on the other. Then, men, women, and children picked up the rope and pulled with all their might. The Hostiles lost, and 298 people left Oraibi and formed the new village of Hotevilla.

In Hotevilla, however, the U.S. government continued to exert its control over the Hopis. Leaders of the new community were imprisoned and the children were forced to go to school.

Hopi children were made to attend boarding school in Keams Canyon. While there, they were required to wear American-style clothing, attend Christian church services, and speak only English. Children caught speaking the Hopi language were slapped or whipped. The children of Hotevilla were treated worse than the other Hopi children. They had to go to school year-round, and in the summer they were sent by the school to work as servants in local Anglo homes.

The children were treated so tragically for two reasons. The first was to punish parents who objected to government policies. The second was to strip the children of their Hopi identity and to replace their world with an Anglo version of it.

There were other programs designed to help the Hopis. These included the building of a hospital; drilling wells for drinking water; digging ditches for irrigation; and "sheep-dipping," giving sheep a medicinal bath to protect them from skin disease.

At the end of the 1920s, the U.S. government began to realize that there were high levels of poverty, malnutrition, and disease on the reservations where thousands of Native Americans were forced to live. When President Franklin D. Roosevelt took office in 1933, he named John Collier to head the BIA. Collier deeply respected the American Indians and was knowledgeable about them.

With Collier's leadership, Congress passed the Indian Reorganization Act (IRA) in an attempt to give some self-government back to the native peoples living on federal reservations. The act allowed each recognized tribe

*John Collier (right), the head of the Bureau of Indian Affairs (1933–45), personally admired Native American culture, but the bureau's policies were still largely disrespectful and harmful to the Hopis.*

to adopt a constitution; set up tribal councils, which would be recognized by the U.S. government; and participate in developing local programs. The underlying message was that traditional ways of life would now be respected and encouraged.

Most Hopis objected strongly to the IRA because they felt that the U.S. government had no business setting the rules for how the tribe should govern its members. When it came time to vote on whether to support the IRA or not, they refused to vote at all, in protest over the whole issue. The majority of those who did vote, however, supported the act, and it passed.

Passage of the IRA caused a second split among the Hopis, this time into two groups known as Progressives and Traditionals. Progressives supported the election of a tribal council, as called for by the IRA. Traditionals wanted the clan chiefs to continue as local leaders. While these two systems of government coexist in Hopi villages today, they do not necessarily cooperate with each other.

In spite of the best intentions of John Collier and the BIA, the programs they implemented in the first half of the 20th century were largely misguided. Policies were put into effect without consulting local councils; serious differences over money owed to the

Hopis arose; and unrealistic programs—such as relocating Native Americans to cities—were failures.

Even promising Congressional legislation—for instance, the 1950 approval of $88 million for worthy projects such as wells, fences, and roads—still represented the U.S. government's interference in Hopi life. Many Hopi leaders continued to object. ▲

*Hopi jewelry, traditionally made by men, is highly valued far and wide. Here, silversmith Eldon Siewiyumptewa, Sr., practices his fine art.*

CHAPTER 6

# "To Guard This Land"

Hopis today find themselves struggling to correct the wrongs they suffered in the past. And they still search for ways to strike the balance that is traditionally so important to Hopi culture. The central issue in these efforts is their land.

In 1949, 24 leaders of the Traditionals sent a letter to authorities in Washington, D.C., expressing their convictions about the importance of land. They wrote,

> This land is the sacred home of the Hopi people. It was given to the Hopi people . . . to guard this land by obedience to our traditional and religious instructions. We have never abandoned our *sovereignty* to any foreign power or nation.

Amid other concerns, such as the illegal selling or stealing of Hopi land, one issue caused particular trouble. The Hopis' next-door neighbors, the Navajos, were moving onto the Hopi reservation. The Navajos' population had grown rapidly and they needed more land. The Hopis feared that if they let the Navajos stay, their rights to that land would be threatened.

The BIA did little to stop the Navajos, on the basis of the exact wording of the 1882 executive order creating the Hopi and adjoining reservations. The land had been set aside for "Hopis and other Indians," and Navajos were other Indians.

In 1950 the Hopis brought their complaints before the Indian Claims Court. Throughout the decade, the Hopis and Navajos negotiated over land rights but made no progress. In 1962 a federal court review ruled that the Hopis had exclusive use of the land under their villages and surrounding them. This amounted to 630,000 acres of the 2.5 million acres originally allocated only 80 years earlier in the executive order. The Hopis and Navajos had "joint and undivided" rights to the remaining 1.9 million acres.

The Hopis mistrusted this ruling because it did not clearly address the problem of Navajos moving onto Hopi land. The Hopis

*Disputes over Hopi land have continued into the 20th century. Hopi and Navajo representatives here try to work out their differences in 1972.*

continued to seek exclusive rights to all their ancestral lands.

In 1974 Congress passed the Navajo-Hopi Settlement Act, which provided for the equal distribution of the remaining 1.9 million acres. But the problems did not stop there.

Both Hopis and Navajos who found themselves on the wrong side of the new boundary lines were given five years to move. This was less difficult for the Hopis since fewer Hopi families were living on Navajo land than vice versa. In 1978 and 1988 amendments to the act provided federal money for relocation and the purchase of additional land for the Navajos. Several hundred Navajos still refused to leave, claiming religious and ancestral ties to the land. In 1993 Congress—in another seemingly imperfect solution—arranged for the Hopis to provide 75-year leases to these families.

Another court battle over land began in 1966, when the Hopi tribal council began leasing land to a number of American companies for the production of oil and gas and the mining of coal and minerals. The Peabody Coal Company was one of the largest of these companies. It negotiated with the tribal council to lease the land for strip-mining in return for $500,000 a year. (Strip-mining is a method of digging for coal that destroys the land as it goes.)

The arrangement between the coal company and the tribal council upset the Traditionalist chiefs. They attempted to bring a lawsuit against Peabody Coal as well as the BIA and the United States Department of the Interior. The chiefs charged that the BIA did not fulfill its responsibility to protect the Indians' lands and rights. To explain the importance of this matter, the chiefs wrote: "If the land is abused, the sacredness of Hopi life will disappear."

*One contemporary, yet traditional, Hopi occupation is sheep ranching. For centuries, Hopis have used their sheep's wool to weave blankets and cloth.*

Land was not the only issue at stake in this dispute. Continuing the disagreement begun in the 1930s, the Traditionalists held that the tribal council had no authority over Hopi land. The council represented only those who had voted in tribal elections, and that was a minority of Hopis. The suit against Peabody Coal was turned down, but the important issue of sovereignty had again been raised.

The Hopis of today do not live in isolation as they once did. While most still live on the reservation, many of them commute daily to jobs off the reservation. It is not uncommon for each family member to help support the household with a combination of working for wages, farming, and raising livestock. On the reservation, traditional crops such as corn, beans, and squash are still grown. Sheep, goats, and dairy and beef cattle are raised.

Despite this, the Hopi Nation faces serious economic problems. Anglos own most of the businesses and run most of the services open to the Hopis. The Hopis are generally hired for low-paying jobs with little responsibility. In the 1970s, however, the tribe opened a center on one of the mesas that includes a motel, restaurant, craft shop, and museum. It has successfully attracted visitors and income.

Hopi arts, including painting, jewelry making, and silversmithing, have become very popular in the United States, but traditional Hopi pottery has experienced the greatest comeback. In 1900, centuries after Hopi women had stopped making traditional pottery, a woman named Nampeyo began studying prehistoric Hopi bowls, dishes, and jars. She led the way in once again using traditional materials and designs, and since then, other Hopis have followed her course.

The Hopi population living on the reservation in 1990 was listed as 7,360: 3,777 men and 3,583 women. These men and women largely remain true to their traditional values in spite of the pressure to adopt Anglo ways. As one 20th-century Hopi spokesperson said, "Our religious teachings are based upon the proper care of our land and the people who live upon it. We must not lose this way of life if we are to remain Hopis, The Peaceful." ▲

# GLOSSARY

**antibody**   a substance in the blood that will protect a person from catching a specific illness

**arid**   extremely dry

**barren**   producing little or no plant life

**conquistadores**   Spanish forces who conquered most of South and Central America and parts of North America in the 16th century

**dune**   a hill of sand created by the wind

**encroach**   to go beyond the proper limits, slowly entering another's property to take possession

**exempt**   free from some requirement that others must face

**forage**   to wander in search of food

**irrigate**   to supply farmland with water

**kiva**   a large, usually circular, underground chamber in which some Pueblo religious ceremonies are held

**mesa**   a flat-topped, tablelike hill that is smaller than a plateau

**mission**   a religious center founded by Christians trying to convert the native population to their faith

**mortar and pestle**   a deep bowllike container (mortar) and a clublike tool (pestle) used to pound or grind materials

**noxious**   physically harmful

**plateau**   a large, high plain that is bigger than a mesa

**ritual**   ceremonial, usually according to religious or social customs

**sovereignty**   freedom to govern one's own nation without outside control

**tainted**   morally corrupted; affected with something bad

**tribute**   arbitrary payment demanded by the group in power

**ward**   a person under the guard or protection of another person or an institution such as a government

# CHRONOLOGY

**ca. 8,000 B.C.** According to archaeological evidence, the Hopis' ancestors first appear in what is now the American Southwest

**A.D. 1300–1400** The Anasazis break up into individual tribes, including the Hopis

**1540** Spanish conquistadores first enter the Southwest

**ca. 1590** Spanish establish permanent colonies in Pueblo territory

**1680** Pueblo siege, led by Popé, drives the Spanish from Santa Fe

**1692** Spanish discover that Hopis have moved to the tops of three mesas

**1700s** Hopis successfully defend themselves against Spanish attacks; a period of relative calm and isolation

**1701** Hopi chief Espeleta leads a raid against Hopi village of Awatovi in retaliation for allowing the return of Spanish priests

**1821** Mexico wins independence from Spain; Pueblo peoples are granted full Mexican citizenship

**1848** The United States acquires Pueblo territory

**1882** Executive order makes Hopi land a protected reservation

**1890** U.S. troops take Hopi children to school by force

**1906** Hostiles lose tug-of-war to Friendlies and leave Oraibi to found Hotevilla

**1934** The U.S. Indian Reorganization Act protects Indian land and allows Native American tribes greater self-government

**1950** The Navajo-Hopi Act gives $88 million for improvement projects on the shared reservation

**1962** Federal court partitions shared Navajo-Hopi reservation

**1966** Traditionalist Hopis denied suit against the Peabody Coal Company, the Bureau of Indian Affairs, and the U.S. Department of the Interior over strip-mining

**1974** The Navajo-Hopi Settlement Act further divides shared land

**1993** Congress arranges 75-year leases for Navajos living on Hopi land

# INDEX

## ABOUT THE AUTHOR

BRYAN P. SEARS is a Baltimore-born writer who was a news reporter for three years. This is his first book about Native Americans. Sears still lives in his hometown with Fitzgerald, his Chesapeake Bay Retriever.

## PICTURE CREDITS